Contents

Note to the Reader
Some words in this book are printed in **bold** type. This shows that the word is listed in the glossary on page 30. The glossary gives a brief explanation of words that might be new to you.

Introduction

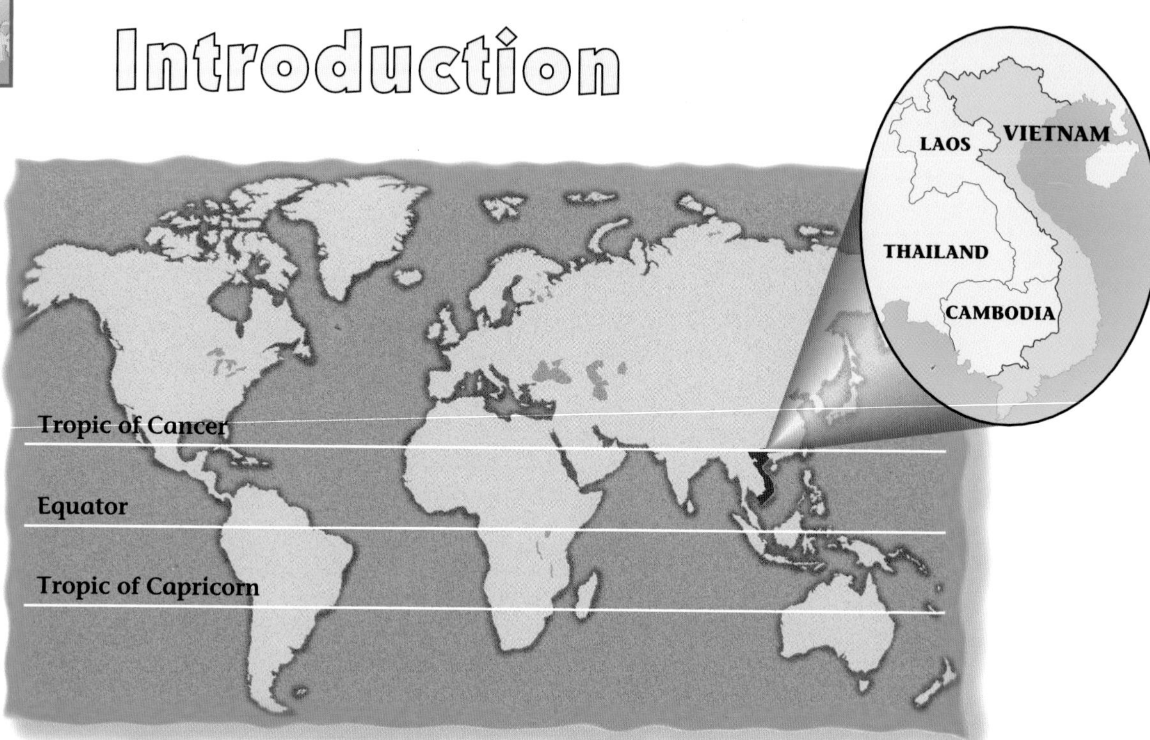

If you had visited Vietnam in 1975, you would have found a country almost ruined by war. In 20 years of war, including nearly 10 years of fighting between U.S. forces and **communist**-ruled north Vietnam, more than 2,500,000 people were killed. Huge areas of forest and farmland were destroyed.

Since 1975, the country has slowly come back to life. Trees and plants have gradually grown back. The people have worked hard to rebuild their beautiful country.

△ Where is Vietnam?

▽ Rice fields and mountains near the border with China.

Geography

Vietnam is a long, thin, S-shaped country in southeast Asia. It is over 1,000 miles long, but only 31 miles wide at its narrowest point.

The Vietnamese often say that their country is like a long bamboo pole, with two great baskets of rice hanging from either end. This is because two of Asia's largest rivers form their **deltas** in Vietnam: the Red River in the north and the Mekong River in the south. The land around the deltas is very fertile, so this is where most of Vietnam's food is grown and where most of its people live.

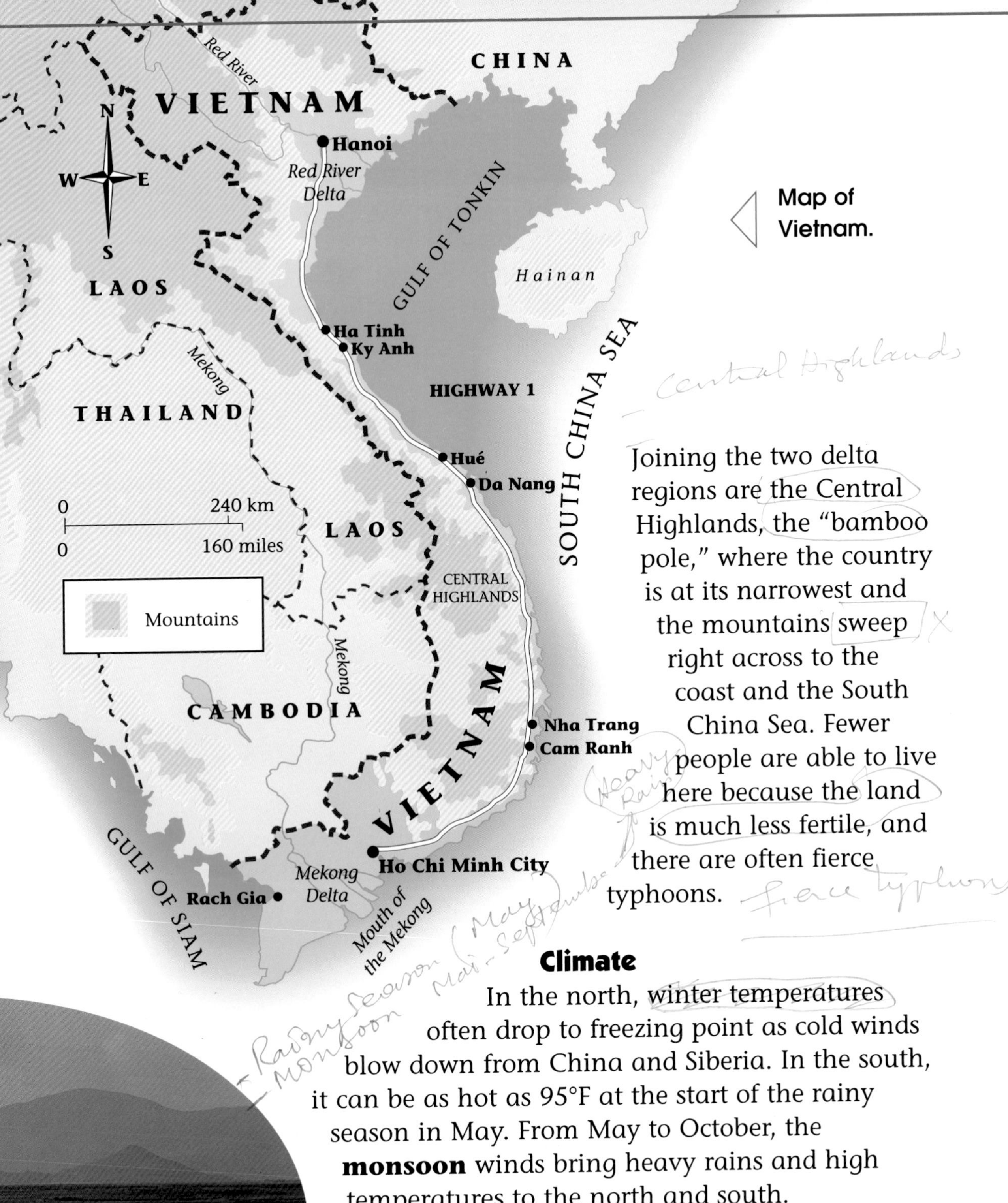

Map of Vietnam.

Joining the two delta regions are the Central Highlands, the "bamboo pole," where the country is at its narrowest and the mountains sweep right across to the coast and the South China Sea. Fewer people are able to live here because the land is much less fertile, and there are often fierce typhoons.

Climate

In the north, winter temperatures often drop to freezing point as cold winds blow down from China and Siberia. In the south, it can be as hot as 95°F at the start of the rainy season in May. From May to October, the **monsoon** winds bring heavy rains and high temperatures to the north and south.

Life can become sticky and uncomfortable during the rainy season, especially for people living in towns and cities, but the whole country depends on the long months of heavy rain. Without them, it would not be possible to grow rice, which is Vietnam's main crop.

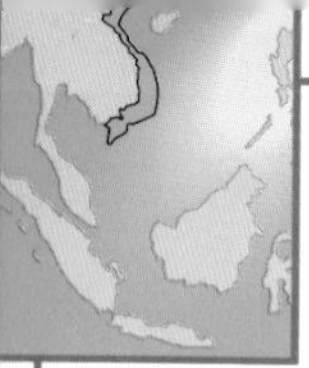

The People

Most Vietnamese people have great love and respect for their families and their country. The oldest son of a family lives with his parents when he grows up and marries, looking after them in their old age. Most homes have a small altar, where the family honors its ancestors.

People also respect their nation and its traditions. They love learning, and shopkeepers, tricycle-taxi drivers, and other workers often relax in the shade with a book when business is slow. Most people's beliefs are influenced by the teachings of **Buddha** and the Chinese philosopher **Confucius**.

A "blackout lantern," used during the war to hide light when bombers flew overhead.

Fighting for Freedom

The history of the Vietnamese people goes back several thousand years. For much of that time they have fought for their freedom.

The main threat has most often been from their giant northern neighbor, China. For a hundred years, until 1954, they were ruled by France. Many older people still speak French as their second language.

Soon after the Vietnamese drove the French out, they were caught up in another, even fiercer, war. Ho Chi Minh, their leader, wanted to run the country as a **communist** state. The United States could not agree to this, because its great rival was the communist Soviet Union. At a meeting of the world's most powerful countries, Vietnam was divided into two separate states. The United States supported the government of South Vietnam in a war against Ho Chi Minh's North Vietnam. The Soviet Union was North Vietnam's ally.

Crowded, bustling streets of Ho Chi Minh City, where American influence is still strong.

The war raged for nearly 20 years, with many people in the South also supporting Ho Chi Minh. The Americans and the South Vietnam army were not able to defeat the North Vietnam army and the thousands of **guerilla** fighters. In 1973 U.S. forces withdrew. Two years later North Vietnamese soldiers marched through South Vietnam, and the country was reunited.

Life Since the War

The years which followed were still very difficult, and most people lived in terrible poverty. Some, the "boat people," were so desperate that they tried to escape across the sea to richer places like Hong Kong.

If you go to Vietnam today, you will find that in most towns the streets are busy and the shops are full. The people hope that Vietnam will soon be as rich as nearby countries like Japan, Thailand, or Singapore.

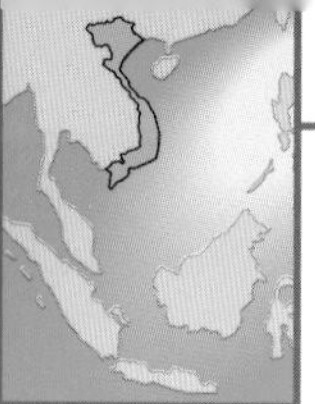

Where Do People Live?

Over 70 million people live in Vietnam. The nation averages 505 people for each square mile; in the United States, the average is about 71 people in the same area.

Cities

Most people live where the land is fertile, around the two river **deltas**. Here, too, are Vietnam's two largest cities: the capital, Hanoi, in the north and the much larger Ho Chi Minh City (formerly known as Saigon) in the south. Though most people are farmers and live in the country, Hanoi and Ho Chi Minh City have nearly seven million people between them.

Both cities are lively, bustling places. Their streets are crowded with bicycles, and their pavements are lined with little booths and busy shops. Hanoi is a city of lakes: at its heart is Hoan Kiem Lake, where people gather to do their exercises before they go to work. Ho Chi Minh City is the country's main business center. It is a prosperous city, but noisy and polluted.

In the crowded cities, family life often flows out onto the pavements.

Halfway along the coast is the old capital city of Hué. Here, on the banks of the Perfume River, emperors of the Nguyen dynasty had their fortress for over 100 years, until 1945. Many tourists visit Hué today to see the emperors' tombs and the beautiful **pagodas**.

Red Dao people from the northern mountains.

In the Mountains

Up in the mountains to the north and west live most of Vietnam's minority tribes—people with different languages and ways of life from those in the lowland regions. They are nearly all farmers. Some live all year round on the land they farm. Others are **semi-nomadic**. Homes here are often quite different from those of most Vietnamese. The Tay people, for example, live in large thatched houses, raised high above the ground on stilts.

Love for the Land

Vietnamese people have always felt great love for their family homes and the land passed down from their ancestors. Over the past 40 years, millions have been forced to leave their homes because of war or poverty. Now they hope that peace and prosperity have come back to Vietnam for good.

Agriculture

If you were flying over the Red River or Mekong **delta** during the rainy season, you would see mile upon mile of brilliant emerald green rice fields. Most Vietnamese people earn their living as rice farmers.

Growing Rice

Planting rice is backbreaking work. The fields have to be flooded, because the young plants will only grow if they are standing in water. The farmers wade ankle-deep through the water, planting each seedling by hand in the mud.

Very few farmers have tractors or other machinery. They use buffaloes to pull their plows. When they have harvested and **threshed** their rice, they often lay the stalks in piles on the road so that cars and trucks will get the last few grains out as they drive over it.

A buffalo plow.

Harvesting rice in the northern mountains.

Overcoming Problems

To grow as much food as the country needs, farmers have to make the best possible use of the land. Most rice fields are surrounded by small earth banks to keep water at the right level, and farmers also dig **irrigation** systems and build **terraces** to make more land available.

Many households raise ducks for their eggs and meat.

In the Red River Delta the land is low, so the river's many branches are liable to overflow their banks. Farmers dig deep drainage ditches to channel the flood water away so that the land does not become waterlogged.

Farmers in many coastal areas have to protect their land from sea floods, especially during the typhoon season. They build great sea walls of mud and stones (sea dikes) to keep the land safe from the huge tidal waves whipped up by the typhoons.

Despite these problems, Vietnam today grows enough rice to feed its own people, and it has a large surplus left over for exporting to other countries. In fact, it is the world's third-largest rice exporter.

Three-quarters of the land in Vietnam is mountainous and cannot be farmed for rice. Farmers up in the hills grow mainly corn and sorghum (a tropical grain).

Although most people in Vietnam enjoy eating meat, few farmers raise cattle or sheep, and people rarely drink milk or eat cheese or butter.

Industry

Most people in Vietnam still work on the land. But their country is going through a time of huge changes. Over the next 20 years, Vietnam is likely to become a far more industrialized country. Fewer than one person in five now earns a living by working in a factory or mine, but soon many more will probably do so.

The blacksmith's workshop is an important center in many villages.

Past Difficulties

One reason for Vietnam's lack of industry is that roads, railroads, and power systems were destroyed by U.S. bombing during the war. Even after the war, it was difficult for Vietnam to repair the damage because of an **embargo** imposed by the United States and its allies. Another reason is that until recently, the government thought that the fairest way to run the country was for all goods to be produced and distributed by the state.

The Huong Canh brickworks supply bricks to cities all over northern Vietnam.

The government tried to build up Vietnam's industry as fast as it could, but people were not allowed to run their own businesses.

This was not an efficient way to run the country. In 1986 the government introduced "doi moi," or "new thinking," which allowed people to start up their own businesses once again.

New Prosperity

Almost overnight, thousands of small businesses, often family-run, sprang up—big and little shops, mechanics' workshops, and small industries. Now that people are allowed to use their business skills again, the country is becoming richer. New industries, such as manufacturing clothes and shoes, are growing.

Vietnam has plenty of mineral resources to help it develop more industry. In the mountains of the north are minerals such as coal, iron ore, and bauxite (from which aluminum is extracted). Huge oil and gas fields lie off the coast.

Many people expect that Vietnam will soon become a richer, more industrialized country. Most Vietnamese, of course, look forward to being able to buy the color televisions and stereos now appearing in their shops. But many are also worried that more factories and mines will lead to more pollution and damage their forests and rich farmland.

△ This community water-powered generator in the northern mountains supplies a whole village with electricity.

Challenges

Wherever you go in Vietnam, people will tell you that life has become steadily better since 1986.

New Freedoms

As a result of "doi moi," people are free to run their own lives and earn their own living as they think best. Before 1986, people worked, not for themselves and their own families, but as members of government-controlled factories or farm **collectives**. Now that they are able to run their own businesses or farm their own land, the country has become richer. With farmers growing rice for their own benefit, crops have increased.

Losses

But there have been losses as well as gains. The **communist** system aimed to share the country's wealth equally among all Vietnamese. Under the new system, many people are richer than they used to be, but some have become poorer.

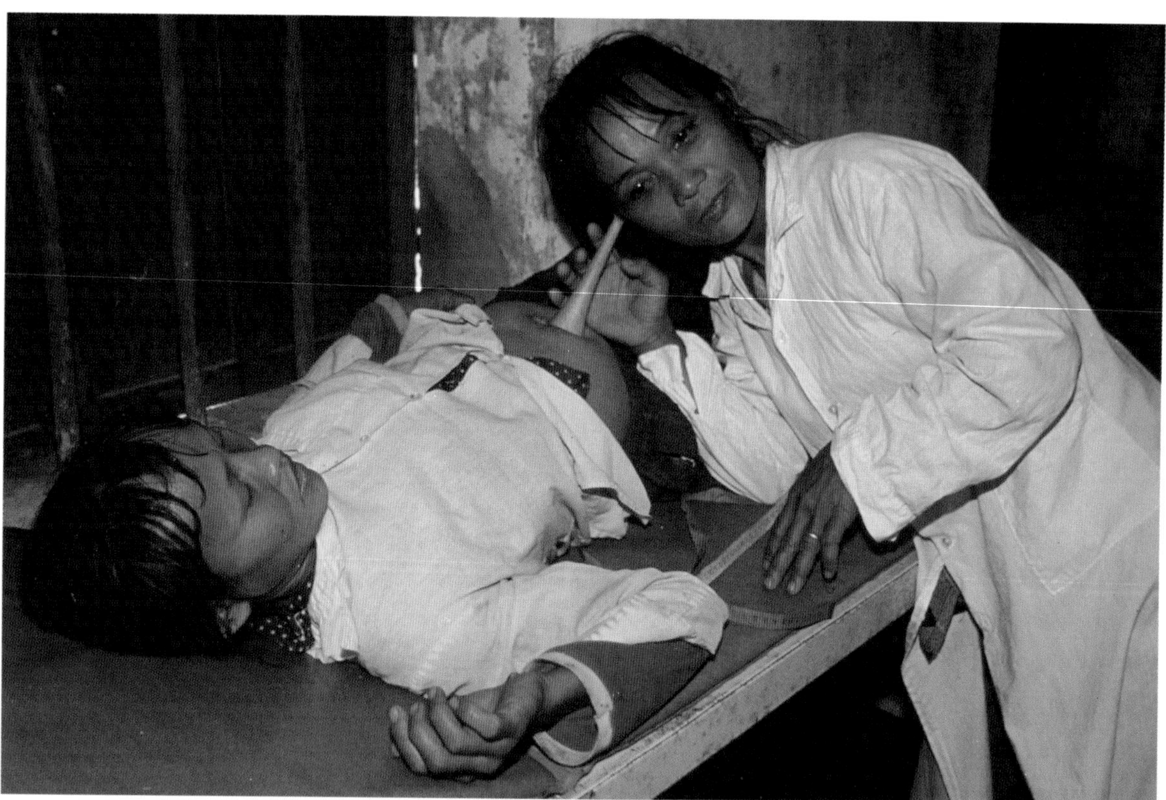

A village midwife in Ky Anh district examines one of her patients.

Children at a state nursery school in Ky Anh town.

Some farmers no longer have enough land to grow food for their families. Many people are unemployed. The gap between the richest and the poorest has grown.

Cutting Services

The government is putting less money into health services, so it is harder for people to get the health care they need. Village clinics are short of drugs and equipment. Most hospital patients now have to pay for treatment; women have to pay to have a baby in a hospital. Some illnesses, such as malaria, are increasing because people are no longer being helped to keep themselves and their families healthy.

Schools have also suffered. Nearly every Vietnamese child used to spend at least five years in school, and most learned to read and write. School was free. Today only the first three years are free, so many families cannot afford to send their children to school. Besides, now they often need them as an extra pair of hands to help in the fields or watch a roadside stand.

The Vietnamese hope that they will now be able to build a richer, stronger country, but many are worried about losing the benefits of the communist system.

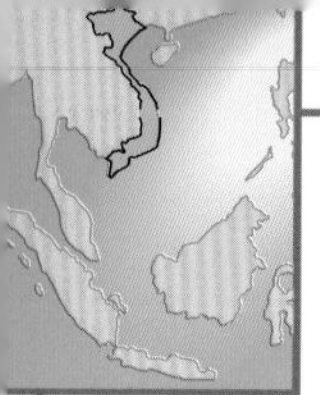

A Farming Community

Nam Ha is one of five villages that make up Ky Ha **commune**. People from these villages know each other well; most people have friends and relatives all over the commune. One village is Catholic, with its own church.

When people are ill or women are expecting a baby, they go to the commune clinic just outside Nam Ha. If they need specialist medical treatment, they are sent to the district hospital in Ky Anh town, or on to the central provincial hospital in Ha Tinh town (see map on page 15).

There are no shops in Nam Ha, but every day there is a small market nearby. People go there from all the commune villages to sell their produce and buy their day-to-day needs. They also use the much larger market in Ky Anh town.

Farming

Just over 200 families live in Nam Ha, 1,800 people in all. Most families depend on farming. Around every home is a large plot, where the family grows sweet potatoes and other vegetables. The village is surrounded by rice fields.

▽ Farmers from all over the district bring their produce to sell in Ky Anh town.

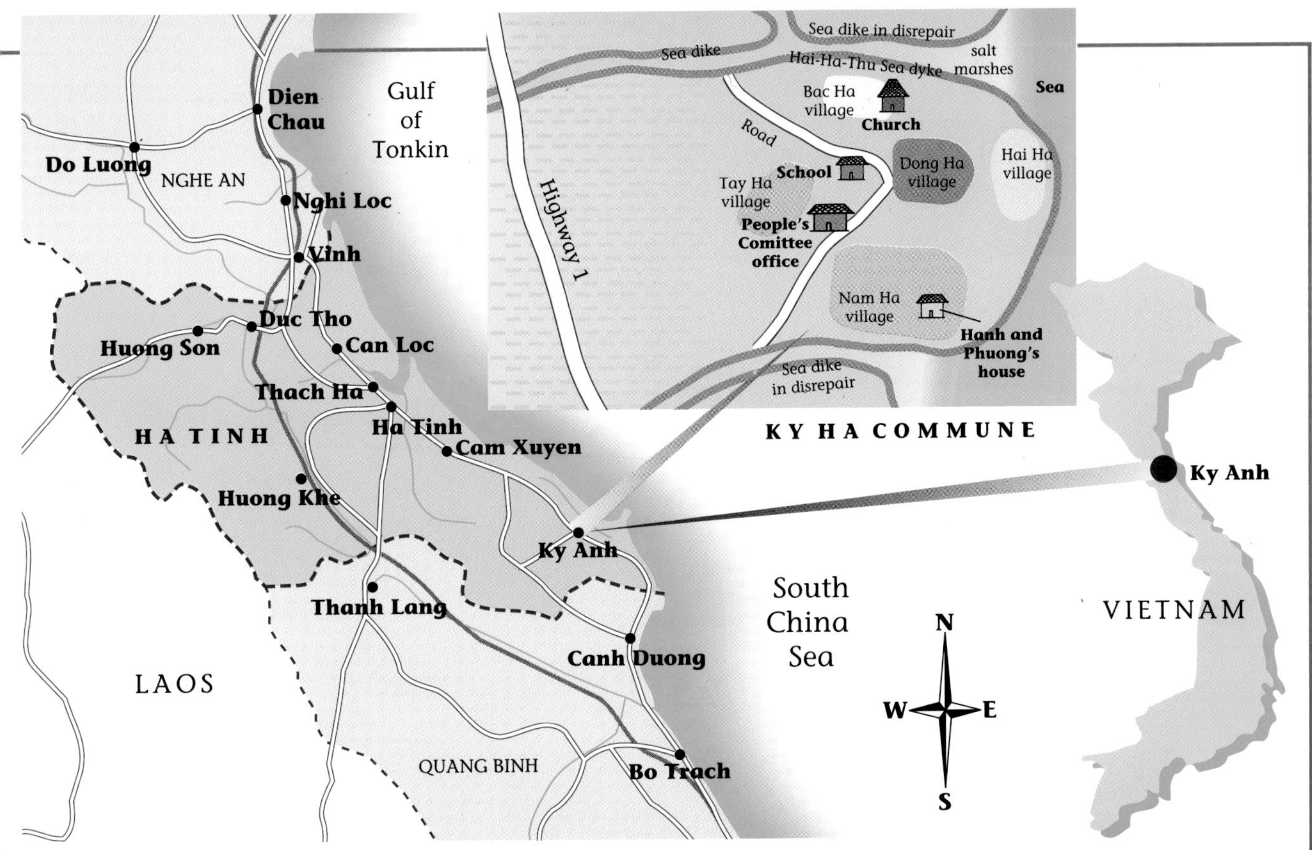

Over the past few years, the state has been giving land back to individual families. Their land still belongs to the state, but they can farm it as they want to. To make the distribution fair, each family was given a mixture of fertile and less fertile land, so their plots are often scattered over a wide area. If a family does not make good use of their plots, they can be given to a more efficient family.

△ Map of Ky Ha commune.

Other Ways to Earn a Living

Some men from the village work as carpenters, builders, or blacksmiths. Several men and women extract salt from sea water during the dry season, or raise fish, shrimp, and crabs in the pools behind the sea dike. They sell the shrimp to a new state-run frozen shrimp factory nearby, which also employs several local people.

About a quarter of the men go south after each harvest to find work for a few months, then come back in time to help with the next harvest. A few have gone abroad, to Russia or Korea. They save as much of their pay as they can so that when they return, they can buy poultry or pigs or start a small business.

Village Life

Nam Ha lies very near the seacoast, in Ky Anh district, one of the poorest districts of Vietnam.

Spreading rice straw out to dry in the sun.

War and Poverty

Ky Anh suffered greatly during the war with the United States. American warships were anchored just off the coast, and people remember that "it was always light here," because all through the night, huge searchlights swept across the land and lit up the sky. The area was often bombarded with artillery fire, and most people from the coastal villages had to be evacuated inland. They were able to return when the war ended in 1975.

In the early 1980s, several harvests failed because of drought and because the old **collective** system was an inefficient way of farming. Many people faced starvation. Most men **migrated** to other areas in search of work. "You rarely saw anyone on the roads," people remember. "Everyone looked weak and sad; no one had any energy."

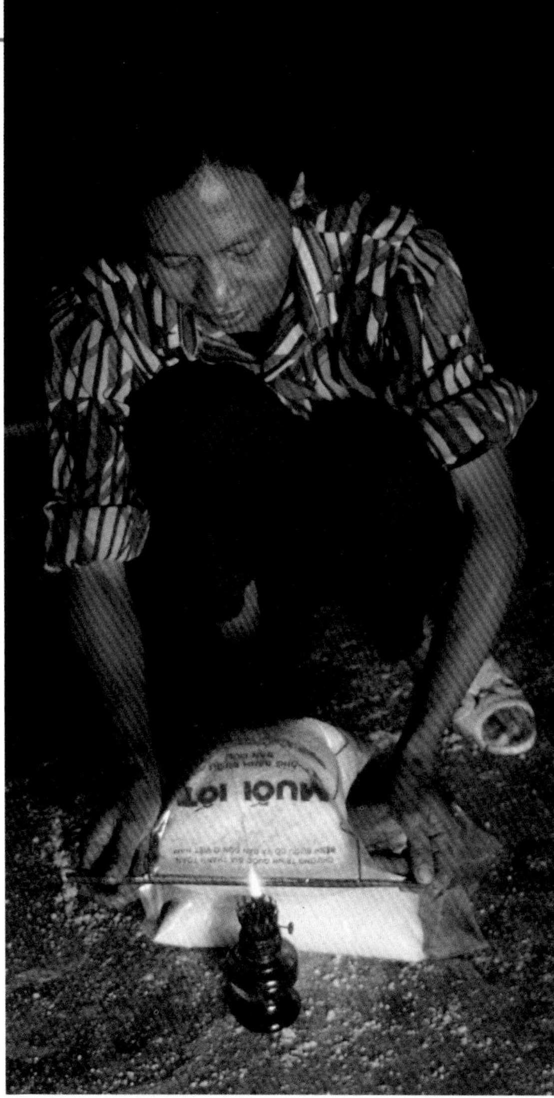

When salt has been extracted from sea water, it is mixed with iodine and sealed into plastic packets.

Life is still difficult for people in Nam Ha and the rest of Ky Anh. The soil is poor, and typhoons often bring huge sea water floods sweeping across the flat rice fields. At other times the land is hit by drought.

Hope for the Future

But people are far more hopeful today. With help from the Vietnamese government and Oxfam, they have repaired the sea dikes which used to protect the land from floods, and they are working to improve and **desalinate** the soil. They are planting trees to break the force of the typhoons and prevent fertile soil from being blown away.

Now that "doi moi" has given them back responsibility for their own plots of land, people can use their skills and knowledge to grow better crops. Many men still spend part of the year away, working in the south of the country, but many of the families who left have been able to return.

In Nam Ha, the Women's Union uses money from Oxfam to give small loans to some of the poorest women to help them start raising chickens, ducks, or pigs. They have to repay their loans within nine months, so that the money can be lent to someone else.

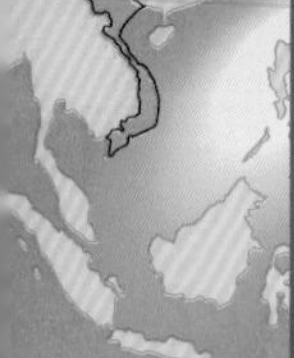

School

Since the end of French rule, Vietnam has built up a very good education system. Most children, even in many of the poorest and most remote areas, are able to go to primary school. Most areas also have good nursery and secondary schools. As a result, nearly nine out of ten Vietnamese adults can read and write, a very high proportion for such a poor country.

Because the government is cutting public spending, parents now have to pay for some of their children's schooling. Some parents in Ky Anh cannot afford to do so and are taking them out of school.

Hanh and Phuong at School

Mrs. Tu is not rich, but like most parents in Nam Ha, she is determined that her two youngest children, Hanh and Phuong, will stay in school as long as possible. "It's our dream that they will go on to high school, and perhaps even to college," she says.

They go to the commune school, just outside Nam Ha. One of their older brothers goes to the high school in Ky Anh town. It is too far to travel each day, so he boards with a local family during the school term.

Hanh and his classmates all wear their Young Pioneer caps, given only to hardworking pupils.

Hanh and Phuong's school has very little equipment, and the walls have no pictures, but the children are all eager to learn. "They work very hard," says Phuong's teacher. There are so many children that they have to be taught in two shifts; half go to school in the morning, and the other half after lunch. Hanh's favorite subject is math; Phuong's is Vietnamese.

Typhoons

Until the sea dikes were repaired, schooling was often interrupted in the typhoon season. Schools were damaged or destroyed by winds and floodwater, and many families had to abandon their homes and flee to higher ground inland. The damaged schools have been rebuilt, and the dikes now protect villages like Nam Ha. Children are able to remain in their homes and continue their schooling.

Children playing outside Nam Ha School in Ky Anh district.

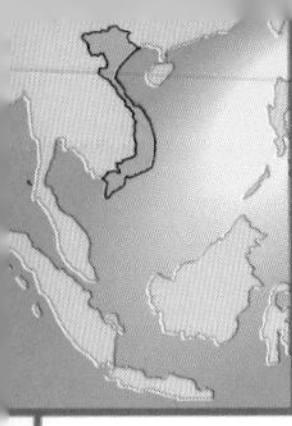

Spare Time

People in Nam Ha work very hard and have little time to relax. Most people make an effort to visit their parents or family on Sundays, especially if they live in a different village.

Festivals

There is no **pagoda** in Nam Ha, and people do not observe religious festivals. Instead they honor their ancestors each day at the small altars in their own homes. Important festivals are Tung Tu, the full moon festival, and the New Year festival of Tet. Tung Tu comes in mid-August, and the whole village spends the day on the beach, singing and dancing. Tet is the occasion for a chess match with a difference: the "pieces" are human beings. They wear their most colorful clothes, especially the "kings" and "queens."

Equally important are Independence Day and International Women's Day. "We get together," says Mrs. Tu, "and celebrate the history of Vietnam and the heroic things people did during the war."

Mrs. Tu (with the pink scarf) hearing about arrangements for a new children's vaccination program in her area.

Many families in Nam Ha enjoy listening to the radio.

Women

In her spare time Mrs. Tu is the head of her local Women's Union. Like all the other Nam Ha women, she attends Union meetings regularly. The meetings are for serious business, like organizing loans to members from the Union's **credit fund**. But they are also a chance for the women to get together and chat.

Children

Though children have to work hard, both in school and at home, they do find time to play. Volleyball and soccer are popular. The boys also play "danh da," competing to throw a coin into a hole. The girls have their own version, "danh vong," played with a small circle of rattan, or cane.

There is no movie theater near Nam Ha, but a few people have battery-powered black-and-white television sets, and one family has a color set. They often invite their neighbors in to watch it, but the children are only allowed to watch on Sunday afternoons, when their homework is done.

A Day with Hanh and Phuong

Hanh is 13 and Phuong is 11. They live with their parents, grandmother, and older sister, Thuy, who is 18 and has left school. They also have an older brother who lives in Ky Anh town and another brother who works in Ho Chi Minh City.

In the main room of their house is a great wooden chest, where the family's rice supply for the whole year is kept. On top of the chest is the altar to their ancestors, with photos of their grandparents and their father's first wife, who died when she was a young woman. Each day they honor their ancestors by lighting incense sticks in front of the photos.

Morning

The family sleeps under mosquito nets to protect them from malaria (a disease carried by mosquitoes). They get up at dawn and wash outside, by the well. Mrs. Tu lights the wood fire in the kitchen and makes noodle soup for breakfast. Hanh and Phuong are both in the morning shift, and go straight off to school. The school is just outside the village, so they walk there with their friends.

After school they help prepare lunch—rice, fish, and vegetables, followed by tiny cups of green tea.

Afternoon

Then they have work to do. Phuong helps her grandmother to weed the sweet potato patch, and Hanh works with his father, feeding the pigs and putting new thatch on the pigsty.

△ Hanh and Phuong washing by the family well.

△ Phuong helps her grandmother in the vegetable patch.

It is harvest time, so rice is spread to dry all over the concrete yard in front of the house. Phuong helps her mother rake it over, so that it can dry more quickly. Then she and Hanh take the family's buffaloes outside the village to graze. They meet several of their friends doing the same job, so they can chat and play together.

There is no electricity in Nam Ha yet, although the poles for the cables are already in place and the Tu family expects to have electric light in their home within a year. The light from the oil lamp is not very powerful, so Hanh and Phuong try to do their homework before dark.

▽ The Tu family's midday meal.

Travel Around Nam Ha

Highway 1 (see map on page 3), from Hanoi to Ho Chi Minh City, cuts right through Ky Anh district. This is the only area in the country where the highway runs close to the coast, so many people think that in the future, tourists will be using it to travel to Ky Anh's beautiful beaches.

At the moment the beaches are empty, and the highway makes little difference to the daily lives of most people in Nam Ha. No one here owns a car, and although buses travel up and down the highway, they do not stop at Nam Ha. When the men who are working away come home, they come by motorbike or hitch a ride on a truck.

Bringing firewood home.

Going to Market

Most people take their surplus crops, or their pigs and chickens, into Ky Anh town to sell. Villagers from Nam Ha have to travel by bicycle or motorbike. Russian motorbikes are very popular here because they are tough and cope well with the potholed tracks around the village. People who have very large loads often use low ox carts or pile their bicycles high and push them.

Earth Tracks

Before the sea dikes were repaired, just traveling from one village to another could be very complicated. Because so much of the land was usually submerged under sea water, travelers had to use ferry boats. Now the tops of the dikes provide tracks wide enough for motorbikes and even cars.

△ **Taking pots to sell in Ky Anh town market.**

Nam Ha is crisscrossed by dirt roads. Out in the paddy fields, the low dividing walls provide dry paths between the flooded fields from one plot of land to another. In and around Nam Ha, most people travel on foot, often carrying heavy loads in two baskets suspended from a pole across their shoulders.

During the three-month rainy season, the tracks are all deep in mud. Traveling out of the village becomes very difficult, and the only way to get anywhere at all is on foot.

Journeys Around Vietnam

Most people in Vietnam travel by bicycle or motorbike, especially in the towns. Many people get around the towns in tricycle-taxis called cyclos. The passenger sits on a seat in front, while the driver sits behind and pedals. Hanoi and Ho Chi Minh City come almost to a standstill during rush hour as thousands of bikes and motorbikes try to force their way along the main highways.

Very few people in Vietnam own cars, so most people traveling around the country go by bus or train.

Buses

Buses are very cheap and go almost everywhere, even into remote mountain areas. But they are very crowded, with narrow wooden seats crammed together. Passengers stand along the aisle, jammed up against each other.

Trucks, buses, and foot passengers board a Red River ferry boat for the five-minute crossing.

This road in northern Vietnam has to be repaired after each rainy season.

The roofs are piled high with luggage, cages of chickens or ducks, and large baskets of vegetables being taken to market.

Even the main roads are full of potholes, and trucks and buses are very old, so they constantly break down. Spare parts are expensive in Vietnam, and often difficult to obtain. Drivers have to be very clever and inventive mechanics.

Trains

Because Vietnam is so long and thin, it has only one main railroad line, which runs between Hanoi and Ho Chi Minh City. It is a single-track railroad, so trains can only pass each other at special passing places. If one train is late, the other just has to wait. And the trains are slow: the journey from Hanoi to Ho Chi Minh City, a distance of 1,078 miles, takes over 40 hours.

Passengers have a choice of "hard seat" (wooden benches) or "soft seat" (with a thin foam rubber covering). Water and tea sellers walk up and down the aisles. The tea sellers carry big kettles covered in polystyrene to keep the water hot and pour green tea into tiny cups. Whenever the train stops, dozens of people swarm on board to sell newly cooked sweet corn, fresh roasted peanuts, baked potatoes, or boiled rice wrapped in banana leaves.

Images of Vietnam

Vietnam

You might expect that after 30 years of war and 20 years of poverty, Vietnam would be a sad and gloomy country.

It is true that you can still see huge areas where the hillsides were burned bare during the war by chemical bombing. And it is true that many Vietnamese, like many Americans, have sad memories of relatives and friends killed in the war.

But over half the people now living in Vietnam have been born since the war. If you visit Vietnam today, you will see people working hard from early morning to late evening and now expecting a better life. You will also see them making time to joke with their children or neighbors, or play a quick game of cards.

◁ **Village hat maker in Nam Ha.**

△ **Buying and selling tapes of traditional Hmong music.**

Water puppets: puppeteers stand behind screens and control the puppets with long sticks under the water.

A Buddhist shrine.

If you visit during the New Year festival of Tet, you will find people really enjoying themselves. They spend days cleaning their houses beforehand, and cooking special food like "banh chung"—a mixture of rice, beans, and fatty pork wrapped in banana leaves. Homes are decorated with peach blossoms to scare off evil spirits. At midnight the noise is deafening, as everyone lets off giant firecrackers to welcome the New Year.

Most people in Vietnam—city dwellers, farmers, tribespeople in the mountains—are proud of their past and their traditions. They are also excited about the future. "Vietnam is coming alive again," they say, and they are working hard to put war and poverty behind them.

Glossary

Buddha Buddha taught that people can find peace and wisdom only when they learn to control their feelings and desires. Buddhists believe in reincarnation, or rebirth.

Collectives *see* Communism.

Commune A group of villages that together make up the smallest unit of government in Vietnam.

Communism A system where land, factories, and businesses are owned and run by the state. People work, not for themselves and their families, but for the community, in large collective farms or factories. Workers in the collectives have to obey government decisions and fit in with government plans.

Confucius Confucius taught that people should put the needs of their community and their nation above their own needs, and that they should respect those who were above them in society.

Credit fund It can be very difficult for poor people to obtain a loan from a bank so that, for example, they can set up a business or start raising pigs. Many join together to pool their savings and set up their own mini-bank. People pay interest when they repay their loans, so the money can help others.

Delta This is land which is formed at a river mouth. As a large river approaches the sea, it divides into many different branches, and some of the material it has been carrying is dumped on the valley floor. This material, called silt, is rich and fertile.

Desalinate Sea water floods leave the soil full of salt, which must be washed out to make it fertile again.

Embargo After the war, the U.S.A. and its allies tried to cut Vietnam off from the rest of the world by preventing other countries from trading with it.

Guerillas Soldiers who fight individually or in small bands. They wage a "hidden" war, attacking suddenly and without warning, then disappear again into hiding.

Irrigation Farmers dig long canals from nearby rivers or lakes to carry water to where it is needed. Children often spend hours scooping water over the banks of the main irrigation canals into their own fields.

Migrated Moved away to live and work in another place.

Monsoon A seasonal wind which occurs in Southeast Asia, bringing very heavy rain.

Pagodas Buddhist temples; in Vietnam they are much smaller than most churches, because people go there mostly for private meditation rather than public ceremonies.

Semi-nomadic People in the mountainous areas of Vietnam who farm by clearing a patch of land and cultivating it for a few years. When the soil becomes less fertile, they move on to another patch and clear that.

Terraces Terraces are small flat areas, like steps, created by farmers on sloping hillsides and supported by low stone and dirt walls.

Threshed When the grain is separated from the stalk of harvested rice.

Index

About Oxfam in Vietnam

Oxfam America works in partnership with communities in Asia, Africa, the Americas, and the Caribbean to find long term solutions to poverty and hunger. Oxfam America supports the self-help efforts of poor people—especially women, landless farm workers, and survivors of war and natural disasters—who are working to make their lives better. Oxfam America believes that all people have the basic rights to earn a living and to have food, shelter, health care, and education.

Oxfam America is part of the international family of Oxfam organizations that work in more than 70 countries. In Vietnam, Oxfam concentrates on three of the country's poorest provinces. Oxfam helps poor communities construct irrigation systems and repair protective sea dikes so that they can increase food production. Working through local women's and farmers' unions, Oxfam makes small loans available for livestock or raw materials to people who are too poor to obtain loans from banks. Oxfam has pioneered the use of typhoon-resistant techniques for buildings such as schools, clinics, and homes, and is working with schools to develop practical environmental forestry programs.

Published by Rigby Interactive Library,
an imprint of Rigby Education,
division of Reed Elsevier, Inc.
500 Coventry Lane
Crystal Lake, IL 60014

Printed in Hong Kong
Designed and produced by Visual Image
Cover design by Threefold Design

00 99 98 97 96
10 9 8 7 6 5 4 3 2 1

Library of Congress Cataloging-in-Publication Data

Simmons, Pat, 1944-
Vietnam / Pat Simmons.
p. cm. -- (Worldfocus)
Includes index.
Summary: Introduces Vietnam through a geographical and historical profile and through case studies of individuals and a representative community.
ISBN 1-57572-026-4 (lib. bdg.)
1. Vietnam--Juvenile literature. [1. Vietnam]
I. Title. II. Series.
DS556.3.S53 1996
959.7--dc20 95-35859

Acknowledgments
The author and publishers would like to thank the following for their help with this book: Oxfam (UK and Ireland): Roger Newton of the South-east Asia Desk; the staff of the photo library; Mary Patience, of Oxfam's Glasgow Education Office, and Teresa Frayn, of Barley Hill School, Thame; Vu Thi Kim Lien, Nguyen Minh Cuong and the staff of the Oxfam Hanoi office; Nguyen Thu Duong; and the people of Ky Anh.

The author and publishers wish to acknowledge, with thanks, the following photographic sources:

Jean-Léi Dugast/Panos Pictures p. 5; ben Fawcett pp. 7, 29a; Tim Page/Eye Ubiquitous p. 29b; all other photographs are by Sean Sprague

Cover photograph: Jean-Léo Dugast/Panos Pictures—Hmong woman and child